FACT CAT

Get your paws on this fantastic new mega-series from Wayland!

Join our Fact Cat on a journey of fun learning about every subject under the sun!

First published in Great Britain in 2015 by Wayland
Copyright © Wayland 2015

All rights reserved
ISBN: 978 0 7502 9581 9
Dewey Number: 941'.01-dc23

10 9 8 7 6 5 4 3 2 1

Wayland
An imprint of Hachette Children's Group
Part of Hodder & Stoughton
Carmelite House
50 Victoria Embankment
London EC4Y 0DZ

An Hachette UK Company
www.hachette.co.uk
www.hachettechildrens.co.uk

A catalogue for this title is available from
the British Library
Printed and bound in China

Produced for Wayland by
White-Thomson Publishing Ltd
www.wtpub.co.uk

Editor: Izzi Howell
Design: Rocket Design (East Anglia) Ltd
Fact Cat illustrations: Shutterstock/Julien Troneur
Other illustrations: Stefan Chabluk
Consultant: Kate Ruttle

Picture and illustration credits:
Alamy: Heritage Image Partnership Ltd cover; Corbis: Heritage Images 4, Stefano Bianchetti 7; iStock: Grigory Fedyukovich 9, TonyBaggett 12, gbrundin 13t, Liz Leyden 18, AndrewJShearer 21; Science Photo Library: Claus Lunau; Shutterstock: jps 8, hramovnick 10, Arne Bramsen 11, Silia Photo 16; Stefan Chabluk 5; Wikimedia: Abbaye de Saint Aubin title and 19, Lorenz Frølich 6, Rob Roy 13b, Berig 14, Jeblad 19, 20; Werner Forman Archive: Courtesy of the Royal Commission on Historical Monuments 15.

Every effort has been made to clear copyright.
Should there be any inadvertent omission,
please apply to the publisher for rectification.

The author, Izzi Howell, is a writer and editor specialising in children's educational publishing.

The consultant, Kate Ruttle, is a literacy expert and SENCO, and teaches in Suffolk.

FACT CAT FACT

There is a question for you to answer on each spread in this book. You can check your answers on page 24.

VIKINGS

Izzi Howell

WAYLAND
www.waylandbooks.co.uk

CONTENTS

THE VIKINGS IN BRITAIN

The Viking way of life started in **Scandinavia**. As the Viking population grew, they started to look for new lands. Explorers found that Britain was a rich country with good farming land. Around 790CE, the Vikings carried out the first **raids** on Britain, which at that time was **ruled** by the **Anglo-Saxons**.

Viking raids were violent. They burned down **monasteries** and villages, and stole treasure.

The Vikings travelled much further than Britain. They went as far east as the country we now call Turkey, and sailed west to North America. What was the name of the first Viking to reach North America?

Over the next 100 years, the Vikings attacked many areas of Britain, and used their large army to take land. At first, the Anglo-Saxons fought back, but in the end, they decided to let the Vikings **settle** in the east of Britain, in an area called the Danelaw.

Land ruled by the Vikings

Land ruled by the Anglo-Saxons

York

Danelaw

This map shows the parts of Britain ruled by the Vikings in 878. As well as the Danelaw, the Vikings also ruled over parts of Scotland and Wales. The Anglo-Saxons ruled the rest of the country.

York was one of the biggest Viking cities in the Danelaw.

VIKING KINGS

In the 900s, people living in the Danelaw followed **laws** made by the Vikings in Scandinavia. In 1013CE, Sweyn Forkbeard, the Viking king of Denmark, invaded England and took control of the Danelaw and the Anglo-Saxon parts of the country.

Sweyn Forkbeard

Sweyn Forkbeard was the first Viking king to rule the whole of England. This painting shows Sweyn at his father's funeral. What was his father's name?

FACT CAT FACT

Sweyn Forkbeard was king of England for just 40 days before he was killed. No one knows who did it, but there are stories that he was killed by a ghost!

Sweyn's son, Cnut, became the second Viking king of England in 1016. Cnut also controlled Denmark, Norway and Sweden, making England part of a large Viking **empire**.

EVERYDAY LIFE

At the time of the Vikings, powerful leaders called jarls owned large areas of land and helped the king to control the country. **Peasant** men, called karls, lived and worked as farmers on the jarls' lands. Karls would also fight for their jarl in battles or raids.

Jarls lived in large buildings called longhouses. Everyone in the area could stay in the jarl's longhouse if the village was attacked.

Most karls lived in small wooden houses near to their farms. Inside each house, there was one room that would be shared by the whole family. This included children, parents and grandparents.

benches

FACT CAT FACT

Many Vikings lived in the countryside, but there were some larger towns and cities. The largest Viking city in Britain was York. What was the Viking name for the city of York?

FOOD

The Vikings grew vegetables and kept animals, such as pigs and sheep, on their farms. Vikings living near rivers and seas would catch fish and seals for food. Some Vikings even managed to catch whales using spears.

Vikings would dry fish outside so that the fish would keep for several months.

On special occasions, there would be a feast in the jarl's longhouse. Lots of different dishes were served at feasts, such as roast meat or fresh fruit. Sometimes the feasts would last for several days, or even a week!

At feasts, Vikings would drink a strong drink called mead from cups made from cow horns. What is mead made from?

FACT CAT FACT

Viking families ate only two meals a day. They would eat their first meal in the middle of the morning, and their second later in the evening.

CRAFTS

In Viking times, village **craftsmen** made everyday objects. Plates, bowls and cups were made from wood. Blacksmiths made simple metal tools and weapons.

Skilled craftsmen made gold and silver jewellery for kings and powerful jarls. These silver Viking chains, rings and brooches were found buried together in northern England.

FACT CAT FACT

Archaeologists sometimes find lots of metal objects buried together. This is called a hoard. The largest Viking hoard found in England had over 8,500 different objects, including coins and jewellery.

The Vikings were excellent **carvers**. They decorated their wooden ships and houses with beautiful designs. They also carved special symbols, called runes, onto stones to show where important people were buried.

Each rune carved around the edge of this stone has a different meaning, such as 'horse' or 'day'. Together, the runes make up a message.

This is one piece of a Viking chess set that was found on a Scottish island. The chess pieces are carved from ivory. Which part of an animal does ivory come from?

RELIGION

The first Vikings that came to Britain on raids were **pagans**. They believed in many different gods and goddesses. There were many famous stories, called myths, about the lives of their gods.

Odin

The Vikings painted this stone with a picture of Odin, the king of the Viking gods, riding his eight-legged horse. What was the name of Odin's horse?

FACT CAT FACT

The Vikings believed that the sound of thunder was made by Thor, the Viking god of thunder, banging his giant hammer.

At the time of the Viking raids, Anglo-Saxon England was a **Christian** country. When the Vikings settled in England, many of them decided to become Christians as well.

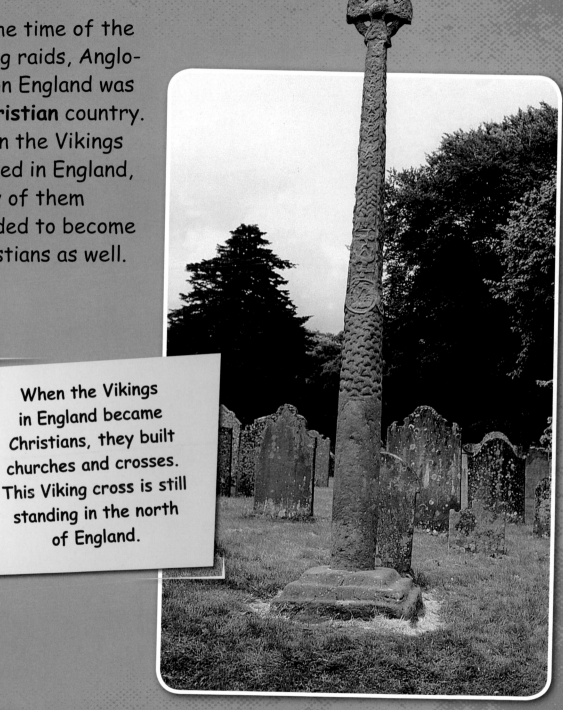

When the Vikings in England became Christians, they built churches and crosses. This Viking cross is still standing in the north of England.

VIKING SHIPS

Vikings travelled in narrow **longships**. These ships could sail across the deep sea and go up shallow rivers. This helped the Vikings get close to towns before starting their attack.

The bow of this **replica** longship is carved into the shape of a dragon's head to scare enemies. What is the back part of a ship called?

bow

During the day, the Vikings may have used sun compasses to find out what direction they were sailing in. At night, the Vikings used the stars to **navigate**.

When the sun shines on the dial in the centre of the compass, it makes a shadow that shows the direction you are travelling in.

sun compass

dial

North

West

shadow

East

South

FACT CAT FACT

The Vikings may have used birds to help them find their way. Most birds don't fly far from land, so if the Vikings saw them, they knew their ships were close to shore.

WEAPONS AND ARMOUR

Every Viking man owned weapons, as fighting was an important part of Viking life. Karls would have used spears or knives. Kings and jarls fought with swords and large axes.

This is what we think Vikings soliders looked like. Viking axes had long handles. Some were over a metre long!

The Vikings used wooden shields to protect themselves in battle. Powerful Viking leaders had expensive metal helmets, but most Viking soldiers wore leather helmets.

This painting shows an army of Viking soldiers travelling to battle in **chain-mail** armour. What type of weapon are the soldiers carrying?

chain-mail armour

This type of metal helmet would have been worn by jarls and kings.

FACT CAT FACT

Many old paintings and drawings show Vikings wearing horned helmets, but there is no evidence that they actually did. Most Vikings helmets were round, as you can see in the pictures on this page.

THE END OF THE VIKINGS

After King Cnut died, his sons, Harold and then Harthacnut, became the next Viking kings of England. When Harthacnut died in 1042, an Anglo-Saxon king, Edward the Confessor, took his place and the Vikings lost control of England.

hare

Cnut's son Harold was known as 'Harefoot' because he was a fast runner. In this drawing, Harold is shown sitting next to a **hare**.

The Anglo-Saxons ruled England from 1042 until the **Norman** invasion in 1066. During this time, some Vikings continued to live in England, but they did not follow Viking laws. Over time, the Viking way of life in England started to disappear.

The Vikings continued to control areas of Scotland until the 15th century. On the Scottish island of Shetland, they celebrate their Viking past by burning a replica longship at a fire festival.

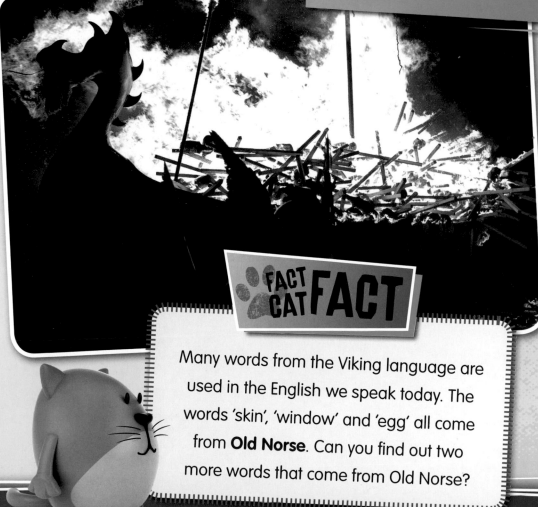

FACT CAT FACT

Many words from the Viking language are used in the English we speak today. The words 'skin', 'window' and 'egg' all come from **Old Norse**. Can you find out two more words that come from Old Norse?

QUIZ

Try to answer the questions below. Look back through the book to help you. Check your answers on page 24.

1 When were the first Viking raids on Britain?

a) 400CE

b) 790CE

c) 878CE

2 Who was the first Viking king of the whole of England?

a) Edward the Confessor

b) Cnut

c) Sweyn Forkbeard

3 In Viking times, jarls owned the land. True or not true?

a) true

b) not true

4 Who was the king of the Viking gods?

a) Odin

b) Thor

c) Harold

5 The bows of Viking longships were carved into the shape of a horse's head. True or not true?

a) true

b) not true

6 Viking helmets had horns. True or not true?

a) true

b) not true

GLOSSARY

Anglo-Saxons a group of people that ruled England after the Romans left in 43CE, originally from northern Germany and Denmark

archaeologist someone who studies objects left behind by people who lived in the past

carver someone who is skilled at cutting designs into stone or other materials

CE (Common Era) after the birth of Christ

chain-mail small metal rings that are joined together to make armour

Christian someone who believes in the Christian religion

craftsman someone who is skilled at making things by hand

empire a group of countries ruled by one leader

hare an animal similar to a large rabbit

law rules followed by everyone living in a country or an area

longship a narrow wooden boat used by the Vikings

monastery a place where religious men, called monks, live together

navigate to find the right direction to travel by using maps or other methods

Normans a group of people from the north of France who invaded England in 1066, and took control of the country

Old Norse the language that was spoken by the Vikings

pagan someone who follows an ancient religion with many different gods

peasant a poor farm worker

powerful able to control people and events

raid a sudden attack

reconstruction a place that has been built to look the same as it would have done in the past

replica an object that has been made to look the same as a historic object

rule to control a country or an area

Scandinavia a region that includes the countries of Sweden, Norway, Denmark, Finland and sometimes Iceland

settle to start living in a new place and make it your home

INDEX

ANSWERS

Pages 5–21

page 4: Leif Ericson

page 6: Harald Bluetooth

page 9: Jorvik

page 11: Honey

page 13: Teeth or tusks

page 14: Sleipnir

page 16: Stern

page 19: Spears

page 21: Some examples include 'Thursday', 'husband' and 'reindeer'

Quiz answers

1   b) 790CE

2   c) Sweyn Forkbeard

3   a) true

4   a) Odin

5   b) not true. They were carved into the shape of a dragon's head.

6   b) not true. Most Viking helmets were round.

EARLY BRITONS TIM...

around 750,000BCE	The British Stone Age begins when early ... in Britain.
2500BCE	The Bronze Age begins in Britain.
800BCE	The British Iron Age starts.
43CE	The Romans invade Britain and take control.
400CE	The Roman army starts to leave Britain as the first Anglo-Saxons arrive.
800CE	Vikings carry out raids along the east coast of England.
878CE	King Alfred the Great gives the Vikings control of the Danelaw.
1013CE	The first Viking king rules England.
1042CE	The Anglo-Saxons take back control of the English throne.
1066CE	The Normans defeat the Anglo-Saxons, and start to rule England.

BCE – The letters BCE stand for 'Before the Common Era'. They refer to dates before the birth of Christ.

CE – The letters CE stand for 'Common Era'. They refer to dates after the birth of Christ.